Great St Mary's is a Church of England parish church in the centre of the city of Cambridge. Welcoming people from many backgrounds and nationalities, it has been at the heart of Cambridge life for over 800 years. The first written record of the church is dated 1205, and it is therefore appropriate that a new guide to the church to commemorate the eight-hundredth anniversary of the event is published, replacing the book which has served parish and visitor well for over thirty years. Today, the church community puts many gifts at the service of the city, the university and the surrounding county of Cambridgeshire.

Great St Mary's has contributed to Christian thought through sermons and sharing in the university's work and celebrations. Copies of recent sermons are available on the bookstall and on the church's website, www.gsm.cam.ac.uk.

One of the clergy is Chaplain to University Staff, managing a chaplaincy centre for members of all faiths on the West Cambridge Site and offering pastoral support to many postdoctoral researchers and others.

Great St Mary's, the University Church, is where town, gown and tourists encounter one another. You may be among the thousands of visitors welcomed each year. Whether you have come to look around the church, climb the tower, to pray or to sit quietly, we hope that you enjoy your visit. In particular, the tower offers a magnificent view of Cambridge, overlooking the market place, the Senate House and the colleges. A member of the church staff is usually at hand to answer any questions. In the north-east corner is St Andrew's Chapel which is set aside for private prayer.

St Michael's Church, a few minutes' walk along Trinity Street, is also in the parish. This is the home of the Michaelhouse Centre, where visitors and others alike can obtain welcome refreshment in congenial surroundings and where mediaeval architecture and a modern ambience mix harmoniously.

John Binns

CONTENTS

Dr John Binns is the Vicar of Great St Mary's

The history of Great St Mary's

John Hammond's map of Cambridge 1592

The origins of Great St Mary's are shrouded in history. Before the Norman Conquest, Cambridge was already a thriving market town. It was razed by marauding Danes in the year 1010. Out of these ashes arose the tower of St Benedict's [Bene't's] church, and probably also a church on a hill by the market place on the site of Great St Mary's. There are written records of the church's existence since 1205; Gervase is listed as the first incumbent the following year.

By then it was probably the largest building in Cambridge, used for public functions and meetings of guilds and other civic organisations. When scholars arrived from Oxford in 1209 and took up residence nearby, they began to use the nave for meetings and the conferment of degrees, the church having the same patron saint as the 'university church' in Oxford. Thus, almost by accident, St Mary's (not yet Great St Mary's but St Mary-by-the-Market) became part of the nascent University of Cambridge.

This church was surrounded by thatched and timber-framed buildings. It is not surprising that it was destroyed by fire in 1291. The re-building was sporadic. The chancel was not re-consecrated until 1351, but it was certainly in use before then. The building was also the centre for the

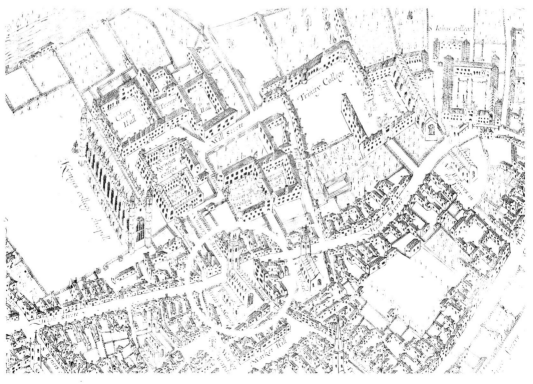

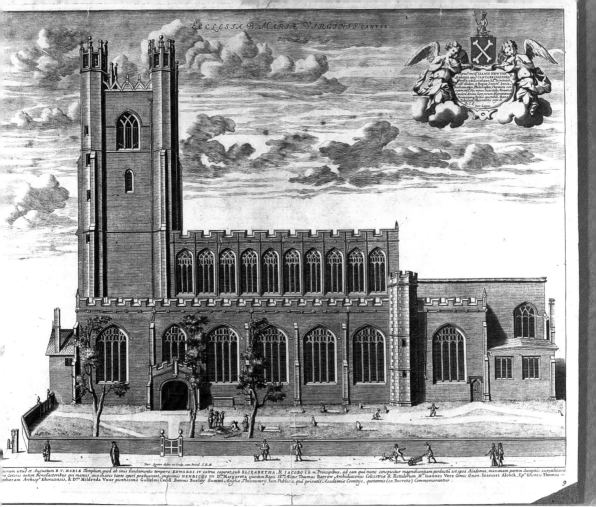

community life of a then more populous parish, where parishioners were baptised, married and were buried, and supported it by their offerings. The right to appoint the Vicar was given to King's Hall in 1342, a right inherited by its successor, Trinity College. In return, the college became responsible for keeping the chancel in good repair.

Feelings between townspeople and the university were often strained, though both used the church for their meetings. This rivalry came to a head in 1381 when townsmen, led by the Mayor, burst into the church, seized the records stored in the University Chest, and burnt them in the market square. This is why the records of the university and of the church before this time are meagre compared with their counterparts in Oxford.

By the time the church had been re-built, it was St Mary 'the Great' to differentiate it from St Mary 'the Less', the old church of St Peter-outside-the-Trumpington-Gate in Trumpington Street which had been re-dedicated in 1352. After little more than a century, the nave of Great St Mary's was either too small or not impressive enough for university purposes. The largest landowner in Cambridgeshire, Richard, Duke of Gloucester, later King Richard III, began the fund-raising in 1475 by donating twenty marks. A further thirty marks allowed the building to start three years later.

Great St Mary's from the south, David Loggan engraving, 1690

left: *Interior looking east, early nineteenth-century, showing box pews, the three-decker pulpit in the nave and Doctors' Gallery in the chancel.*

right: *Martin Bucer (1491–1551), reformer. He was buried in Great St Mary's but his body was exhumed and burnt at the stake in Queen Mary's reign. (See page 28)*

Under Richard's successor, King Henry VII, building resumed after money had been donated by priors, abbots and doctors and masters at the university whose names are commemorated in windows around the church. By 1519, the re-building of the Nave was complete. It had cost about £1,350. Work on the new tower had reached only the height of the nave. Not until the 1590s did work start to complete it, the tower achieving its present form in 1608.

In the mid-sixteenth century came the Reformation. In 1549 Divine Service was performed in English for the first time in Great St Mary's. The glory of the late-mediaeval church, glowing in colour with windows filled with stained glass, wall-paintings of biblical scenes and a painted and gilded roof, was, within sixty years, transformed into a plain, whitewashed auditorium with only its architecture reminding the congregation of more colourful times. Although the nearby St Edward's church claims to be the 'cradle of the

Great St Mary's from the west, eighteenth-century drawing

*Ground plan of
the nave c.1820,
showing central
pulpit and
seating*

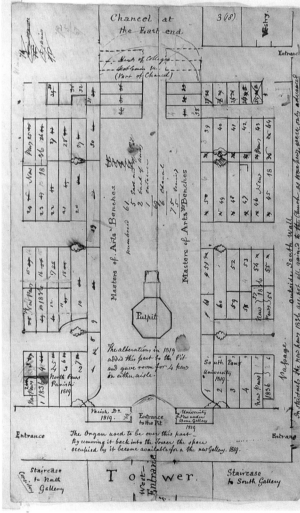

English Reformation', many of the Cambridge reformers preached from Great St Mary's pulpit. Thirty-five of them perished at the stake in the reign of the Roman Catholic Queen Mary between 1553 and 1558.

As well as serving as the University Church, Great St Mary's continued to function as a parish and civic church.

Seats for the mayor and aldermen were placed in the chancel facing westwards towards the pulpit. The affairs of parish, university, diocese and a teeming market town were crowded together on a constricted site. Shops, not demolished until 1767, abutted the west wall of the church, jutting out into the High Street (King's Parade), which was itself only twenty five feet wide. Every year, it was necessary to cart away quantities of 'filthe about the churche', and frankincense was used inside to drown the stench. When Elizabeth I visited Great St Mary's in 1564, twenty loads of sand were spread over the churchyard to cover mud and rubbish.

Religious dispute continued to be played out inside the church, even after the 'Elizabethan settlement' brought about a measure of religious harmony. Noteworthy, was the conflict between Thomas Cartwright, the Lady Margaret Professor of Divinity, a Puritan, whose sermons often filled the church to overflowing, and John Whitgift, the Master of Trinity College, a more moderate churchman. Eventually, Cartwright was deprived of his chair, banished from the university, and became the founder of English Presbyterianism.

This heralded a change to a new style of churchmanship. During the late 1630s, the altar was placed against the east wall of the church with an altar rail in front of it. Parishioners' seats were removed from the chancel and a new and costly rood screen was built across the chancel arch. For a few years a style of ceremonial worship not witnessed in the church since before the Reformation and not seen again until the nineteenth century prevailed.

After the Puritan Long Parliament met in 1640, Great St Mary's became, once again, a place where preaching predominated. The early eighteenth century became the first age of the formal university sermon. The aisle galleries and the three-decker oak pulpit were installed in the 1730s, a chancel gallery in 1754 and a west gallery in front of the organ in 1837. All Bachelors of Divinity living in Cambridge as well as Masters of Arts in holy orders were required to preach in turn. By this same time, the function of the church as a meeting place of the university had come to an end with the opening of Gibbs's Senate House in 1730.

The late eighteenth and early nineteenth centuries saw further changes in religious thought and practice. Evangelical preachers were then drawing huge crowds to the church (approximately one in five of the entire Cambridge population) as were high churchman, now almost forgotten, like Bishops Marsh of Peterborough and Kaye of Lincoln. The later Tractarian movement, with its emphasis on reverence and the sacraments, was prompting a general dissatisfaction with the eighteenth-century style of worship. When Henry Luard became vicar of Great St Mary's

Henry Richards Luard, Vicar 1860–87 (top), and William Cunningham, Vicar, 1887–1908 (below)

in 1860 he received support from the university and (less so) from the parish to return the church more nearly to its mediaeval form. The chancel and west galleries were removed, the three-decker pulpit was dismantled and carved stalls were installed in the chancel and fixed pews in the nave. Following a fire which destroyed the houses adjoining the east end of the church, a new east window was installed and the outside of the chancel refaced. Early the following century a war memorial commemorating those soldiers from Cambridge killed in the Boer War

'MR' Maria Regina, monogram in the railings (see page 20)

*Nave looking
west c.1860.
Eighteenth-
century pulpit
and Edward
Blore's west
gallery*

between 1899 and 1902 was placed below it on the outside of the church.

Luard's successor, William Cunningham, was of a different persuasion. From a free-church background, and having taught at the evangelical Jesus Lane Sunday School, Cunningham was a noted economic historian. He had travelled widely, and his awareness of the worldwide Anglican communion made the congregation – parish and university members alike – aware of the church's pastoral responsibilities. He was also a controversialist on political and economic matters. Cunningham was vicar into the twentieth century, but he was essentially a nineteenth-century figure who, with Luard, established a role for the church for the century ahead.

Their spiritual successor was Mervyn Stockwood, the first vicar for many centuries who had not been a

Fellow of Trinity College. Like them, he was a controversialist, who recognised, when he was appointed in 1955, that the world was changing. He believed that questions about the nature of human understanding, whether religious or secular, should be aired from the pulpit and not just in university common rooms. Soon after his appointment he established the 8.30 pm Sunday evening university service, which endured for thirty years. Some of the sermons at these services were later published in book form. When well-known personalities like Mother Teresa of Calcutta and Billy Graham preached they filled the church to capacity. On the same Sunday as the first of these sermons, Stockwood introduced the first Parish Eucharist.

Mervyn Stockwood, Vicar 1955–9, greeting students after a university service

Stockwood was vicar for only four years. His legacy lived on, but by the 1980s it was obvious that the 8.30 pm service had run its course. A new vision of Great St Mary's as a city-centre church, stretching out to city, university and visitors alike, began to take shape. Since then, the expansion of the university has led to the appointment of a Chaplain to University Staff, who is also a member of the church's ministry team. The development and transformation of the nearby St Michael's church into a thriving community and café facility, the Michaelhouse Centre, has been accomplished. Finally, worship through music has become an integral part of the life of the church. What the future will bring to Great St Mary's, situated physically and figuratively between 'town and gown', will be for God and future generations to decide.

left: *Edward Blore's design for a spire c.1820. A spire was intended when the tower was built in the sixteenth century*

A walk around the church

The tower

A visit to Cambridge by John Wastell in 1491 marked the re-commencement of work on King's College Chapel and the tower of Great St Mary's. Facing each other on Senate House Hill, both are constructed externally of oolitic limestone with a soft local stone inside to facilitate carving. The building of the tower was to take nearly 120 years; in 1536, after the installation of the west window, work ceased for nearly sixty years, and the tower was given a thatched roof which was later replaced by slates from the dissolved nearby Austin Friars. The bells had been hung inside the tower on a temporary frame and the ground floor probably served the dual purpose of a ringing chamber and a robing room. On either side were extensions to the nave aisles entered through small arches. These are now the kitchen and the church office. A room in the north-west corner of the church functioned as the Consistory Court where, until 1948, minor moral and ecclesiastical cases were tried. The court also convened to consider proposed alterations to church buildings.

Why then did the building of the tower begin again in 1592? Despite an economic recession, this was a time of national euphoria and many church buildings were being restored and beautified. Advances in the art of bell ringing precipitated the re-building of church towers to house ringing chambers and peals of bells. A flurry of fund-raising – which included two shillings from each university student, five shillings from each commoner, and ten shillings from each fellow – enabled the tower of Great St Mary's to be raised another twenty-four feet. Over a period of two years, more than

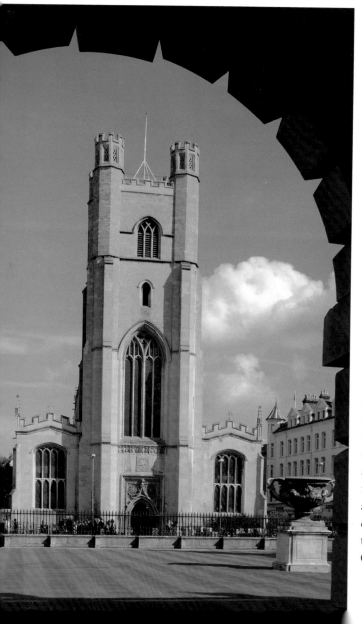

The milestones

On the outside of the tower, near the west door, is a circular plaque. This marks the datum point established in 1732 by Dr William Warren, a Fellow of Trinity Hall, as the centre of Cambridge. From this point, using a sixty-six foot chain, he measured three roads out of Cambridge placing milestones along them, many of which still survive. The work was paid for out of a highways charity set up by Fellows of Trinity Hall and Gonville and Caius. The Master and Fellows of Trinity Hall were the trustees of the charity, which is why the milestones are marked with that college's coat of arms. Like all university fellows of the early eighteenth century, Warren was a clergyman, and it was no coincidence that he chose the spiritual centre of the town as its physical centre from which to measure distances.

The clock

The first clock in the tower was donated in 1577 by Dr John Hatcher, the Regius Professor of Physic who was the university Vice-Chancellor two years later. When the university installed a new clock in 1793, Joseph Jowett, the Professor of Civil Law was asked to produce suitable chimes. He was probably assisted by William Crotch who later became a distinguished composer of church music. The chimes, properly known as the Cambridge Quarters, are said to be based on an extract from Handel's 'I know that my Redeemer Liveth'. Adopted for Big Ben for the newly-built Houses of Parliament in 1858, they are now familiar as the Westminster Chimes. The dial on the outside of the tower dates from 1679 and the present clock was bought in 1892 as a memorial to the Revd. H. P. Luard, Vicar of Great St Mary's from 1860 to 1887

£219 was spent on construction. Robert Grumbold, whose family later built St John's College Library and the Wren Library of Trinity College, was the master-mason.

In 1593, the belfry was added, and, fifteen years later, the tower reached its present height of a hundred and fourteen feet. By this time, fund-raising had slowed down, and a proposed eighty-foot spire, rivalling that of the University Church in Oxford, was never built. Work ended, however, on a sad note. John Warren, a churchwarden, was killed when he fell from the tower. What happened is not recorded, but, in those days, churchwardens were responsible for the direct supervision of the builders. No longer does the west window allow light into the church as originally intended; when the West Gallery was erected in 1837, the University Organ was moved into the tower itself and obscured the window altogether.

BENEFACTORS TO THIS PARISH

THOMAS JAKENETT formerly a Burgess of this Town, and Agnes his Wife. Anno 1469 Founded Four Alms Houses adjoining the south side of this Church yard, which were afterwards increased by this Parish to Eight. These Houses being taken down in consequence of an Act of Parliament granted in the Year 1788 for Paving and improving the Town of Cambridge, were Rebuilt on a piece of Ground at the end of Walls Lane adjoining to Christ College Pieces, at the joint expence of the University and the inhabitants of this Parish in the Year 1790.

JOSEPH MERRILL Gentleman many Years an inhabitant of this Parish at his Decease in the Year 1805, bequeathed to the Trustees of Storey's Charity Cambridge the sum of 1667 Pounds Stock in the 3 Per Cent Consolidated Bank Annuities. IN TRUST that they cause the Dividends arising from the same (deducting Two Pounds per Annum for the expences of the Trust) to be distributed half Yearly to such eight poor Persons as have been elected by this Parish into the aforesaid Alms Houses

The bequest boards

Against the walls of the narthex and in the galleries are painted boards which record bequests to the church. Benefactions range from quite modest to large sums, showing that the perception of Christian duty was to care for the needy, provide sums for the purchase and distribution of food, clothes or coal, set up schools for the teaching of poor children and provide alms houses for the elderly.

The bells

It is recorded that, before the building of the present church, bells were hung in a wooden structure in the churchyard when its predecessor was demolished. In 1515, this was dismantled and the bells placed in the as yet uncompleted tower. These may not have been rung very often, as, in 1564, the church was fined for 'not ringing at the Queen's coming'. In 1593, four bells were installed into a new belfry where visitors can still see bells today. This was the occasion of prolonged rejoicing by the congregation: all the bells 'rung out as never before'. In 1611, a new bell was added, a sixth in 1622, and a further two completed an octave in 1668. There was obviously an enthusiastic band of bell ringers, so that, by the early eighteenth century, the bells and their fittings were showing signs of wear. In 1722, the old bells were lowered from the tower, melted down, and replaced by a new ring of ten. With two more added later, the possible number of changes was raised to 479,001,600 – thirty-three years' continuous ringing. The replacement of the old bells provided the opportunity to formalise the bell ringing team, and, in 1724, the Society of Cambridge Youths came into existence; the identity of every single bell ringer from that time, with his or her occupation, is recorded. It gave the opportunity for a new ringing chamber to be constructed only ten feet – three metres – below the bells themselves, which gave the bell ringers greater control over the swinging bells. In the 1950s the bells were re-hung on a steel frame in the now conventional clockwise order. In 1879, the University Guild of Change Ringers was founded, and, for the first time, there was a formal split between parish and university bell ringers. Today, the Guild rings for the 9.30 am Sunday morning service in term and the Society out of term. Membership of the Society continually hovers around the thirty-mark, consisting of a wide range of age and occupations, from those who are no longer in the first flush of youth to young children, learning the art of campanology on hand bells.

The nave

While King's College Chapel, retains much of its late-mediaeval splendour, the inside of Great St Mary's is plain by comparison. Only by observing the arch soaring in 'celestial symmetry' above the chancel step can one envisage Wastell's original concept. Originally, suspended beneath the arch, dominating the entire nave, was a giant crucifix, with the figures of the Virgin Mary and St John on either side of it. Below the crucifix was a screen, probably spanning the whole width of the church, partially concealing a view of the chancel. In the aisles, behind parclose screens were side-chapels dedicated to various saints. By visiting Wastell's two other churches – at Saffron Walden and Lavenham – the visitor can see how the church might have appeared before the installation of the galleries in the eighteenth century. Underneath the galleries, on either side of the chancel arch, are dark oak screens, consisting of panels from the eighteenth-century three-decker

Interior of nave, looking west towards the tower entrance

pulpit, which was the dominant feature of the nave for more than a hundred years. The screen on the north side leads into the sole remaining mediaeval chapel, which is dedicated to St Andrew. Its counterpart on the south side is the entrance to the church vestry, previously the Lady Chapel.

Light and space, with soaring arches pointing heavenwards, were the essence of late-mediaeval architecture. Without the balance of stained-glass windows, images and wall-paintings, this might have given rise to a cavernous and austere appearance. In Great St Mary's the unlikely combination of eighteenth-century galleries and nineteenth-century pews has replaced the chapels and decorations intrinsic to Wastell's original vision. Twentieth-century stained glass and modern images have enhanced this.

The roof

Along the centre line of the roof at the points where the ribs intersect, large bosses contain a number of figure carvings – the Virgin Mary as Queen of Heaven, St Michael fighting the dragon, a pelican-in-its piety symbolising Christ, a priest kneeling before a crucifix, two demi-angels holding a star, and the Crown of Thorns. These, because of their height and relative inaccessibility, escaped the wrath of the reformers. In fact, this remarkable roof owes its creation to an act of regal larceny and its survival to an early example of conservation. In 1506, that most parsimonious of monarchs, King Henry VII, donated oak trees from an estate he did not own at Great Chesterford, about twelve miles from Cambridge. Nearly three hundred

Sixteenth-century carved roof bosses: the Pelican-in-its-Piety; a priest kneeling before the crucified Christ; St Michael fighting Satan in the form of a dragon

opposite: the north gallery and clerestory

years later when this roof was showing signs of decay, James Essex, a local architect who was responsible for many college buildings, decided, instead of replacing it, to build a new roof above the old and tie the two together.

The *Te Deum* windows

The stained glass in the re-built Great St Mary's fell victim to the sixteenth-century iconoclasts. But, if the visitor looks upwards to the clerestory, a succession of stained-glass windows can be seen, each based on a verse from the *Te Deum*. These were inserted between 1902 and 1904, from specifications by the vicar, William Cunningham. In all, sixty figures are portrayed, placed in a roughly chronological sequence from west to

left, clockwise: *Te Deum windows*
– Old Testament prophets: Jonah, Ezekiel, Daniel
– Martyrs of the early church: Margaret, Catherine, Agnes
– Apostles (with the features of contemporary churchmen): Matthew, Thomas, James

east along the north side of the church and then from east to west along the south. The 'glorious company of the apostles, the goodly fellowship of prophets and the noble army of martyrs' are depicted, showing the history of Salvation from the beginning to the christianisation of eastern England. The figures on the north side take the viewer from the Old Testament to the New, from Abraham to the apostles. The faces of some of the apostles are adapted from portraits of Victorian clergymen who preached in the church – F. J. A. Hort, B. F. Westcott, J. B. Lightfoot, E. H. Stanley, J. F. D. Maurice and Thomas

Arnold. On the south side, are portraits of the apostles, through the martyrs of the early Church to later saints such as St Edward the Confessor, St Alban and St Edmund. The light of Christ's revelation shines through these 'lights of the world in their several generations' on to the congregation below.

The font

Before the Reformation, fonts were usually painted or carved with religious images. Considered superstitious by the iconoclasts, these were mostly destroyed. This may have

been the reason why, in 1620, the churchwardens of Great St Mary's were fined for not keeping the font in good repair. Three pounds were donated towards a new font, on which religious imagery was presciently absent, enabling it to survive the puritan 'cleansing' of the church twenty years later. Its style and shape are Jacobean Gothic with Renaissance decoration. The octagonal shape represents the seven-

Seventeenth-century font with date: 1632

Nineteenth-century movable pulpit

day weekly cycle, with the 'eighth' day representing eternity. Its position near the entrance is a reminder that baptism is the means of entry into the Church. During the eighteenth century, when the church was principally a 'preaching box', the font was placed out of sight beneath the staircase leading to the Doctors' Gallery. By the 1840s, this was a constant cause of complaint, few people being able to gather around it and in 1862 it was moved to its present position.

The pulpits

It would be tempting to believe that the present pulpit was the one from which the great figures of the English Reformation preached. Unfortunately, this is not so. The mediaeval pulpit was replaced in 1618 by a pulpit which is now in Orton Waterville church near Peterborough. It appears that this was originally in the centre of the nave, but was moved to the first south pillar during the Laudian reaction twenty years later. It was replaced in 1736 by a 'three-decker pulpit' of black oak, from which the preacher, after disappearing through a door at its base, 'rose up like a slow jack-in-a-box'. The middle desk was reserved for the minister when reading prayers and the lower desk was used by the parish clerk. Like its predecessors, it was situated in the middle of the church but faced east towards the chancel. It was the dominant feature of the church for a hundred and thirty years, being moved towards the west end of the church when the new gallery was installed there in 1837. By the 1840s, it was no longer held that the pulpit should be 'the central object on which every eye is to be fixed'. In 1863, it was dismantled, and its panels were later brought back to the church to be used in the west arches of St Andrew's chapel and what is now the vestry. When the present pulpit, was installed by the university on the north side of the chancel arch in 1872, it led to

complaints that the preacher could not be seen from many parts of the church. The solution was to install rails so that it became a movable pulpit, enabling it to be moved into the centre of the church for university sermons.

The galleries

Central to the teaching of theology in the eighteenth century was the sermon. Students were advised to hear and make abridgements of two sermons each Sunday and holy day. There were insufficient seats in the nave, and large numbers of students were forced to stand in the aisles. In his will, in 1709, William Wort, who is buried in the north aisle of the church, left £3,000 for the construction of galleries so that students might 'more

decently and conveniently hear the sermon'. The galleries, above the north and south aisles, were not built until 1735, when interest had added another £1,500 to the original bequest. By this means, 476 additional seats, for the use of undergraduates and Bachelors of Art were added. As a result of a decline in parish income due to buildings being demolished to accommodate the new Senate House, the university agreed to accept responsibility for the maintenance of the galleries 'for ever'. By the mid-nineteenth century, however, the galleries were seldom full as Great St Mary's was no longer the only place to hear sermons. They were, though, needed for big occasions, and Luard, when re-organising the inside of the church in the 1860s, had to acknowledge that they were an

Eighteenth-century south gallery, set into the sixteenth-century arcade

The Blessed Virgin Mary

It is appropriate that a church dedicated to the Virgin Mary has imagery of her inside and outside its walls. In particular, she and St John the Evangelist were prominent on the mediaeval rood screen of Great St Mary's, an image which is now depicted on the wooden processional cross. The roof bosses are all that remain of the mediaeval imagery, some of which show a demi-angel holding a shield with a crowned monogram, MR, Maria Regina. This monogram has been incorporated into the railings around the churchyard together with a white lily which symbolises her virginity. Just inside the entrance to the church, is a small wooden statue of the Virgin and Child, carved by Loughnan Pendred and given to the church in 1962. Beneath her feet is a serpent representing 'that old serpent called the Devil'. In the final cosmic battle, the Devil will be overcome, and will be 'trodden down beneath the feet of the righteous':

'indispensable eyesore'. This is essentially the situation that exists today. When the new Parish Organ was installed in 1990, space was found behind it for a new vestry office. This was essentially an extension of the south gallery, and a glazed screen engraved by David Peace was installed between the two.

The icon near the entrance into St Andrew's Chapel was painted by the icon painter, Patricia Fostiropoulos. This is a traditional portrayal of Mary as the *Hodegetria* or the one who shows the way. Mary holds the Christ Child on her knee with one arm while the other points toward him.

The Parish Chest, benches and pews

The church accounts of 1522 refer to a 'hatch', which is probably the chest now in the south-east corner of the nave. Although much-restored, this is early Tudor, and chests such as this were used to store parish records until comparatively recent times, when records were transferred to county archive offices. Pews and benches first made their appearance in English churches in the late-fourteenth century in response to the increase in preaching. Those members of the congregation who had not brought their own folding stools often moved around the church while listening to the sermon. The first mention of pews or benches in the church is itemised in the churchwardens' accounts of 1510–11 for 'stoles in the body of the chirche'. Sets of pews were rented to members of the congregation from as early as 1537, each costing 16 (old) pence. The poppy-head ends to some of these may survive on the heavy oak, backless benches found

The lily in the railings (see panel above)

right: *poppy-head pew end of the late-sixteenth or early-seventeenth century*

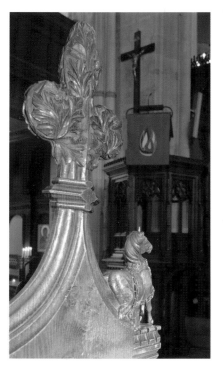

at the back of the galleries which probably date from the early seventeenth century. Twenty-two of these survive. Shortly after the erection of the aisle galleries and of the three-decker pulpit, the university agreed to pay the parish £100 towards the re-pewing of the nave in Norway oak. Parishioners' box pews and backless benches for the Masters of Art were constructed.

Almost a century later, however, these eighteenth-century furnishings were being referred to as 'an alteration so sadly characteristic of the dreariest period in English history'. They were swept away during the church restoration of 1863 and replaced by the present open pews facing eastwards, towards the rising sun, the symbol of Christ's resurrection. The style of these was based on late-mediaeval East Anglian benches with ornate poppyhead tops and animals depicted below them. The inflexibility of these pews became a problem when the pattern of church worship began to change in the 1950s. Two rows were then removed from the front and the back of the nave to provide more open space.

top left: *Brass memorial to Michael Woolf, chuchwarden and landlord of the Rose Tavern, died 1614*

lower left: *Brass memorial to Dr Lorkin, Regius Professor of Medicine in the university, died 1591*

Memorial brasses and tombstones

Three memorial brasses can be seen on the north-aisle wall. These date from the early seventeenth century, and are in memory of three members of the church. They represent the wide diversity of Cambridge residents who have worshipped within its walls. The first is in honour of Michael Woolf, the landlord of the Rose Tavern in the market place and a churchwarden. The next is of Dr Thomas Lorkin, Regius Professor of Physic (medicine) for twenty-eight years, and a Fellow of Peterhouse. In the seventeenth century, women were rarely honoured with a memorial brass unless they were of noble birth. But the third brass is to Ann Scot, the wife of the Public Notary, John Scot. After giving birth to nine children, she died in childbirth while bearing the tenth.

Set in the floor of the Nave is a number of tombstones or vault-covers. Before the mid-nineteenth century, burials below the floor of churches were common, the fees being a welcome contribution to parish finances. When the practice was discouraged on sanitary grounds, many of the vaults were filled in.

Eighteenth-century inscription on a stone originally containing a late-mediaeval brass memorial

St Andrew's Chapel

This chapel, where either the Daily Office is said or Holy Communion celebrated each day, is reserved for prayer and private contemplation, and is where the Holy Sacrament is reserved. Dominating the chapel is the figure of the Risen Christ, by the Hungarian sculptor, Gabrielle Bollobas. It shows Christ rising from the dead, suggesting 'weightlessness and floating'. On the wall beside it is an empty cross carved by a member of Great St Mary's congregation, the late Gordon Steele, which bears the impress of the body of Christ. The modern tapestry in the chapel may, at first, appear to be designed as a simple landscape scene. On closer inspection, it is seen to suggest the road leading from Creation, through God's covenant with Noah, to Salvation through the cross of Christ. The chapel was re-ordered in 1983 using money given in memory of Dr Erwin Loewenfeld, the Church Treasurer from 1944 to 1975.

above: *Figure of the Risen Christ, by Gabrielle Bollobas*

above: *Modern tapestry in St Andrew's chapel*

right: *View into St Andrew's chapel, showing the cross above the altar and the icon of the Virgin and Child (see page 20)*

The chancel

View of the chancel steps, showing the Eagle Lectern and the position of the pulpit rails

At the chancel step, the visitor is probably aware of the contrast between the spacious loftiness of the nave and ahead the more constrained chancel and sanctuary. The latter were restored in the 1850s 'on the old foundation'. Niches on the east wall were re-constructed; although it is not known which saints stood in them, the Virgin Mary was undoubtedly one of them. The lower north and south walls of the chancel are the only parts left standing of the church the present one replaced; the bricked-in arch on the south wall indicates its probable height. On this side also are the arched recesses of a sedilia and double piscina which were uncovered when the wooden panels installed in 1663 were removed. These indicate that the floor of the pre-fifteenth century church was about two feet below the present one.

The gallery placed over the chancel between 1610 and 1616 was dismantled only seven years later; the so-called Doctors' Gallery was installed in the same place in 1754. An armchair ('the Throne') reserved for the Vice-Chancellor was set in the centre of the front row with the royal coat of arms on the wall above it. When Holy

above: *View into the chancel, with nineteenth-century choir stalls and east window, and twentieth-century 'Majestas' sculpture*

right: *The Gilbert Scott reredos of 1865*

Communion was being celebrated, the celebrant had to speak loudly to be audible in the nave. Almost as soon as it was built, the gallery attracted adverse criticism, that it was not 'decent' for those sitting there to have their backs to the altar. In 1863, it was removed and, two years later, a carved alabaster reredos, designed by Gilbert Scott, was installed behind a new

The Butler Memorial

Standing high on the north wall of the chancel is the memorial to Dr William Butler who died in 1618. Besides being one of the most eminent medical men of his time, Butler was a Fellow of Clare College and regularly attended Great St Mary's. He was 'endowed in very rich measure with those qualities of amiable eccentricity that are traditionally associated with University dons', once attempting to cure a patient by having him thrown into the River Thames, then an open sewer. It is doubtful, however, that he resorted to such measures when he was called upon to attend King James I when the king was thrown from his horse at Newmarket!

communion table. In the centre of the reredos was the crucifixion with, on one side, Samuel among the prophets and, on the other, St Paul preaching in Athens. Stalls were erected along the north and south walls, reaching almost up to the east end, to accommodate the heads of houses, professors and doctors displaced from the Doctors' Gallery. In 1872, with the installation of the movable pulpit, they were re-accommodated in the front pews of the nave facing east. The easternmost stalls were removed to create the present sanctuary with the remainder being used by the parish choir founded two years earlier.

In 1958, to simplify the chancel, the reredos was removed and replaced by the 'Majestas'. Images, which had been placed in the niches on the east wall, were taken down, and the altar brought forward and situated behind the sanctuary step so that Holy Communion could be celebrated facing the congregation. This gave the chancel its present appearance apart from the intallation of the new Parish Organ in 1990.

The 'Majestas'

Carved in wood and gilded, 'Majestas' (properly *Majestas Christi*, the Majesty of Christ) was executed by Alan Durst and dedicated in 1960 in memory of the Revd. C. L. Hubert-Powell (Vicar of Great St Mary's from 1914 to 1927) and his wife. Placed above the High Altar, it forms the focus of the church, instantly attracting the attention of the visitor, with its imagery taken from the Revelation of St John. The robed figure of the resurrected Christ stands in front of the cross; his right hand is raised in a gesture of blessing, and his left holds a book. The wounds on his hands and feet are marked with crosses as a reminder of 'those glorious scars' still borne by the risen and ascended Christ. Above him is the crown of his kingship and of eternal

The 'Majestas', carved by Alan Durst

life. On the arms of the cross are the first and last letters of the Greek alphabet – alpha and omega – taken from the words of Christ in Revelation: 'I am the Alpha and the Omega, the beginning and the ending, the first and the last'.

In the angles formed by the arms of the cross are four creatures – a lion, a calf, a man and an eagle – which Revelation describes as surrounding the throne of God. These are the symbols of the four Evangelists, whose writings conveyed the good news about Christ to humanity. Beneath the cross is a serpent, the symbol of Satan and of the evil which has been overcome by Christ's death on the cross. On the book in Christ's left hand is written, *folia ligni ad sanitatem gentium*, 'the leaves of the tree for the healing of the nations'.

The Eagle Lectern

The splendid wooden eagle lectern on the chancel step was given to Great St Mary's by a churchwarden, William Hattersley, in 1867. It is a free interpretation of the many surviving late-mediaeval brass lecterns in parish churches. The symbolism of the eagle is complex. It is associated with St John the Evangelist, whose Gospel sees most clearly into the divinity of Christ as the eagle is able to gaze directly into the sun. When old, the eagle flies directly towards the sun, which would then burn away the deposit of age and renew its youth. The eagle, therefore,

has been used from early Christian times as a symbol of resurrection, both of Christ and the faithful Christian. The globe beneath the eagle represents the world from which he is rising as he gazes at the divine nature of Christ. He, like the Gospel, is turned towards Christ and towards the world.

below: The nineteenth-century Eagle Lectern

The Easter Sepulchre

On the north wall of the chancel is an arch framing a recess, probably built as a monument to John of Cambridge, a prominent lawyer who died in 1335. In the Middle Ages, all churches had Easter Sepulchres, though not all were permanent structures; some of these had carved scenes of the resurrection and ascension of Christ or, as was likely in Great St Mary's, painted images. During the Good Friday service, the consecrated bread was taken in procession through the church before being deposited in a shrine-like cupboard in the sepulchre to symbolise the burial of Christ in the tomb. A watch of prayer was then kept until the midnight vigil on Holy Saturday when it would be returned to the High Altar to the proclamation: 'He is not here; he is risen'.

Martin Bucer

On the south side of the High Altar is a brass plate marking the original burial place of Martin Bucer. During the Reformation Bucer attempted to mediate between warring religious factions. Even before arriving in Cambridge as Regius Professor of Divinity in 1550, he had had a profound influence on those who were to determine the future course of the Reformation, including Thomas Cranmer. He died the following winter, and 3,000 people attended his funeral in Great St Mary's. Six years later, however, the religious climate had changed. The church was placed under an interdict while his body and that of Paul Fagius who had been buried in St Michael's were exhumed. The university Vice-Chancellor, Dr Andrew Perne, preached while the coffins and their contents were burnt to ashes in the market place as the country people manning the market stalls looked on in wry amusement. Perne was to preach again two years later after the accession of Queen Elizabeth I when a ceremony was held in Great St Mary's to re-inter Bucer's supposed ashes by the side of the altar. Perne, of course, became a by-word for religious inconsistency and opportunism. By careful diplomacy, however, he saved many members of the university from persecution under Queen Mary.

The East Window

Installed in 1872, the glass in this window comes from the factory of William Chance who had undertaken research into colouring techniques used by mediaeval glaziers. It illustrates the nativity, with Mary and the child Jesus at its centre. Surrounding this are illustrations of the Christmas story from the conception of Jesus to the flight into Egypt, the upper tracery portraying the hosts of heaven. The window's layout contains a cross, formed by the intersection of the movement from right and left of the shepherds and wise men towards Christ, with the movement downwards from heaven through the child to the angel announcing his birth to the shepherds. The scenes at the bottom of the window read from left to right, illustrating what happened before and after the birth of Jesus. The first scene shows the Annunciation; the next is the Visitation. The remaining scenes show what follows the birth of Christ. In the presentation in the Temple, the child is greeted by Simeon and Anna as the prophesied Redeemer. The narrative is completed by the Holy Family's flight into Egypt.

The small upper lights of the window portray angels surrounding the star which both heralded the coming of Christ and signified Christ himself. The star is in the topmost light and, surrounded by the cloud which veils the ineffable presence of God, shines with its rays on the nativity scene below. Angels represent the hosts of heaven surrounding the throne of God.

The East Window showing scenes from the Nativity of Christ

The organs and choir

Few churches are in a position to provide the setting for a double-organ concerto. Great St Mary's is one of them due to a disagreement over whether the parish or the university should pay for repairs to what is now termed the University Organ. There was an organ in the church in the early sixteenth century, but, by 1584, this had become unplayable, and its case and pipes were sold for one pound nearly thirty years later. There appears to have been no organ in the church for over a hundred years. In 1697, the parish agreed to a university proposal

The 'Father Smith' organ, (the 'University Organ') installed in 1697

that an organ should be erected 'at the only cost and charge to the university'. This organ was bought from St James' Church, Piccadilly, in London, and installed on a wooden gallery at the west end of the church by 'Father' Bernard Smith, the King's organ maker. It was agreed that this should be used for parish and university alike. When the west gallery was installed in 1837, the organ was moved to its present position. In 1869, despite a major renovation, the parish wrote to the university about its poor condition, adding that a subscription had been opened for a parish organ to be installed in the chancel. With the failure to agree on an organ adequate for the requirements of the parish and the university, the shared use of the organ came to an end. Within two years, the University Organ had been repaired and enlarged at a cost of £620, and a small parish organ had been installed in the chancel. This was later reconstructed to a form which was to last for a hundred years. By 1990, it had reached the end of its useful life and an appeal was launched to replace it. In October the following year an inaugural recital was given on a new instrument built by Kenneth Jones of Bray and Associates in Ireland.

When the first Parish Organ was installed in 1870, and stalls erected along the north and south walls of the chancel, a new parish choir of boys and men was formed. Until this time, there had been only a university choir which sang from the west gallery

The modern Parish Organ in the chancel

during university services. The new Parish Choir sang at the main services of Mattins and Evensong, and also provided boys to sing as part of the university choir, an arrangement that existed until the dissolution of the university choir in the 1940s. During the 1950s, the Parish Choir was directed by Dr Douglas Fox who, despite having lost an arm during the First World War, was an accomplished organist and pianoforte recitalist, using his elbow and two feet pedalling simultaneously to make up for the lost arm. Twenty years later, under one of his successors, Graham Sudbury, the choir produced its first recording, *The Sounds of Great St Mary's*, and, augmented by several schools' choirs, sang the St Matthew Passion in King's College Chapel. By this time, the choir was singing at the Parish Eucharist as well as at Mattins and Evensong, a burden which was eased considerably when the Girls' Choir was founded in 1989. Today, the choirs continue to sing separately, but sometimes join together on special occasions.

The Michaelhouse Centre

By the 1980s, a new vision for Great St Mary's had begun to emerge. Gone were the days of radicalism and experimentation. A new ministry for the church, reaching out to townspeople, university members and visitors alike in the centre of Cambridge took its place. Central to this ministry was the transformation of St Michael's Church into the Michaelhouse Centre, which opened in December 2001.

St Michael's was, until 1908, Great St Mary's neighbouring parish along Trinity Street. The church is, in fact, the older of the two, having been re-built in the 'decorated' Gothic style by Harvey de Stanton, Chancellor to King Edward II, in 1324. Besides being a parish church, it was used as a college chapel by Gonville and Caius College and by Michaelhouse (which was absorbed into Trinity College in 1546) until these colleges built their own chapels. In the sixteenth century John Fisher, then Chancellor of the university, and the reformer Paul Fagius worshipped here. St Michael's continued to be used as a parish church until it was united with Great St Mary's. It was then used mainly for children's services on Sundays. On several occasions, there were discussions about its possible use for other purposes. In 1963, however, the vicar, Hugh Montefiore, decided that Great St Mary's needed a parish hall, and £11,000 was raised to make the necessary alterations.

Although they were to suffice for the next twenty five years, these did not meet with everybody's approval. Sir John Betjeman claimed they were an expensive way of ruining a beautiful building. A grander vision for St Michael's afterwards took shape: to restore the church to its former glory and provide rooms and facilities which are versatile and well-equipped for the benefit of a diverse community. It took twelve years and £1.3 million for this to materialise. The café and gallery, a central part of the Michaelhouse ministry, is open from 9.30 am to 5 pm from Monday to Saturday. The Centre hosts a wealth of community activities, including meetings, concerts and plays. The chancel and historic Hervey de Stanton Chantry Chapel serve as places for quiet reflection in the busy city centre. A glass screen allows people in the café to see the extensively refurbished chancel, where contemporary worship takes place during the week. Sunday is generally given over to parish activities, providing a venue for coffee after the 9.30 Parish Eucharist, services for younger members of the congregation and meetings of the Youth Group.